Great
Australian
Paintings

Great Australian Paintings

LANSDOWNE PRESS

Published by Lansdowne Press
37 Little Bourke Street, Melbourne, Vic. 3000
First Published 1971
© 1971 Lansdowne Press
Reprinted 1972, 1974 & 1975
Produced by John Currey
Typeset in Australia by
Dudley E King, Melbourne
Printed and bound by
Leefung-Asco Printers Limited, Hong Kong
ISBN 0 7018 0258 8

Jacket: Arthur Streeton *The Purple Noon's Transparent Might*

LIST OF PLATES

INTRODUCTION

Within the relatively short span of two hundred years, Australian painting has begun to establish a heritage. The first distinctly 'Australian' school of painting came out of the golden era of the 1880s and 1890s. It was the forerunner of a tradition which has continued, even through the modernist phases of art, to the present day.

From the earliest times, movements in Australian painting have been connected with discoveries. The very first visiting painters were discoverers (often in the literal sense, since many were naval men on voyages of exploration). To a curious Europe they sent back titillating glimpses of this strange 'new' continent, its native peoples and its unique flora and fauna. Their paintings were works of record: topographical studies, portraits and 'views' of an alien land. In retrospect their views seem distorted. To our eyes the colonial artists often only succeeded in making the Australian landscape look much like parts of rural England.

The first real discoverers needed the light of the French Impressionist movement to equip them with a true vision of the country. Only in the 1880s, with the arrival in Australia of the *plein air* techniques of modern French painting, did men like Tom Roberts, Frederick McCubbin and Arthur Streeton finally break away from the idealised interpretations which had made up much of Australian painting to that time.

Not surprisingly, the paintings which have already established for themselves a permanent place in the Australian heritage are usually landscapes—like Streeton's *Purple Noon*—which depict the 'typical' Australian countryside or works which in some other way express an aspect of the Australian character. This is the common denominator which links such otherwise markedly distinct and unrelated paintings as Buvelot's *Winter Morning near Heidelberg* and Boyd's *Wimmera Landscape*.

When young European art students like Julian Ashton, Charles Conder and Girolamo Nerli came to Australia they were, in varying degrees, disciples of a new creed: that paintings should not be made wholly within the confines of the studio, but at the scene itself, as the French Impressionists and their forerunners had taught. And when these artists and their colleagues set up their outdoor camps in Melbourne and Sydney they not only discovered a new way of painting but something about Australian life. From the Heidelberg painters sprang a new school of bush genre painting, something particularly Australian, which put on canvas the things that men like Henry Lawson, A. B. Paterson and the bush balladists were writing about.

The bush genre was represented by painters like Tom Roberts, 'the father of Australian landscape painting', who travelled with drovers and depicted, in paintings like *The Breakaway*, everyday life on the stations and shearing sheds of the New South Wales outback; Frederick McCubbin, whose large canvases *The Pioneers* and *Down on His Luck* brought to life with stunning realism the hardships and tragedies of pioneering life in the blue-gum forests of southern Victoria. It was this new understanding of the Australian bush that led young Arthur Streeton to discover that the true colours of the Australian landscape were not autumnal greens and browns but blue and gold. It led Hans Heysen in South Australia to discover that the majestic eucalypt was not just a tree but a thing of beauty.

The Australian impressionists formed the first national school of painting; it is fitting that their works have remained among the most popular in Australian art.

There is a second group of painters whose works gained almost immediate popularity and whose names are equally synonymous with the art of Australia. They too, were discoverers. In the early

INTRODUCTION nineteen forties, Russell Drysdale (*The Rabbiters*) discovered the desolate interior of the continent; the great brooding menacing emptiness which other painters had neglected for more than one hundred and eighty years. His contemporary, William Dobell, discovered the urban Australian; in Dobell's portraits of *The Strapper* and *The Billy Boy*, ordinary Australians could see something of themselves. Sali Herman (*Paddington*) painted the back streets of run-down inner suburbs, the backdrop against which these ordinary people played out their own version of the struggles against adversity depicted by McCubbin sixty years earlier.

This book presents some of the works of these innovators. It is not the story of Australian painting, or an attempt at classification of the best Australian painting. Rather, it is a salute to the founders of the Australian tradition.

Brief notes on the plates reproduced on the following pages, together with details of media, measurements and present whereabouts of the works, will be found in the section at the end of the book.

The editors and publishers greatly appreciate the assistance given by the galleries and individuals who own the works included in this book and who have given their permission for them to be reproduced. Full acknowledgements are included in the notes.

PLATE I Conrad Martens *Sydney from Vaucluse*

PLATE 2 Louis Buvelot *Winter Morning near Heidelberg*
PLATE 3 Louis Buvelot *WannonFalls*

PLATE 4 Frederick McCubbin *The Letter*

PLATE 5   Tom Roberts *The Artists' Camp*

PLATE 6 Frederick McCubbin *The Lost Child*

PLATE 7   Girolamo Nerli *The Voyagers*

PLATE 8   Girolamo Nerli *The Beach at Port Melbourne from the Foreshore, St Kilda*
PLATE 9   Tom Roberts *Coming South*

PLATE 10   Arthur Streeton *Golden Summer*
PLATE 11   Tom Roberts *The Sunny South*

PLATE 12   Tom Roberts *A Summer Morning's Tiff*

PLATE 13   Charles Conder *Departure of the* S.S. Orient—*Circular Quay*

PLATE 14   Charles Conder *Cove on the Hawkesbury*

PLATE 15   Frederick McCubbin *Down on his Luck*

PLATE 16   Julian Ashton *The Prospector*

PLATE 17   Charles Conder *Holiday at Mentone*

PLATE 19   Arthur Streeton '*Still Glides the Stream, and Shall Forever Glide*'

PLATE 20   Frederick McCubbin *A Bush Burial*
PLATE 21   Arthur Streeton *The Selector's Hut*

PLATE 18 Arthur Streeton *Twilight Pastoral*

PLATE 22   Charles Conder *Yarding Sheep*

PLATE 23   Charles Conder *Ricketts Point, near Sandringham*
PLATE 24   Arthur Streeton *Beach Scene*

PLATE 25 Emanuel Phillips Fox *Moonrise, Heidelberg*

PLATE 26 Frederick McCubbin *The North Wind*　　　PLATE 27 Albert Henry Fullwood *The Station Boundary*

PLATE 28　Tom Roberts *The Breakaway*

PLATE 29　Arthur Streeton 'Fire's On', *Lapstone Tunnel*

PLATE 30   Girolamo Nerli *A Wet Evening*

PLATE 31   Tom Roberts *Portrait of Arthur Streeton*

PLATE 32   Walter Withers *A Bright Winter's Morn*

PLATE 33   Arthur Streeton *Boys Bathing, Heidelberg*

PLATE 34   Tom Roberts *Eileen*

PLATE 35 David Davies *Moonrise, Templestowe*

PLATE 36 Walter Withers *Mining Scene, Creswick*

PLATE 37   Tom Roberts *Bailed Up*

PLATE 38   Emanuel Phillips Fox *Art Students*

PLATE 39   Walter Withers *The Coming Storm*

PLATE 40   Frederick McCubbin *Cottage, Macedon*

PLATE 41   Arthur Streeton 'The Purple Noon's Transparent Might'

PLATE 42   Arthur Streeton *The Old Inn, Richmond*

PLATE 43   John Longstaff *Gippsland, Sunday Night, February 20th, 1898*

PLATE 44   Julian Ashton *The Selection*

PLATE 45   Frederick McCubbin *The Pioneer*

PLATE 46   Rupert Bunny *The Garden Bench*

PLATE 47   Elioth Gruner *Australian Landscape: After Frost*

PLATE 48   Hans Heysen *Spring Early Morning*

PLATE 49   Sali Herman *Potts Point*

PLATE 50   William Dobell *Mrs South Kensington*

PLATE 51   Russell Drysdale *The Rabbiters*

PLATE 52   William Dobell *The Billy Boy*

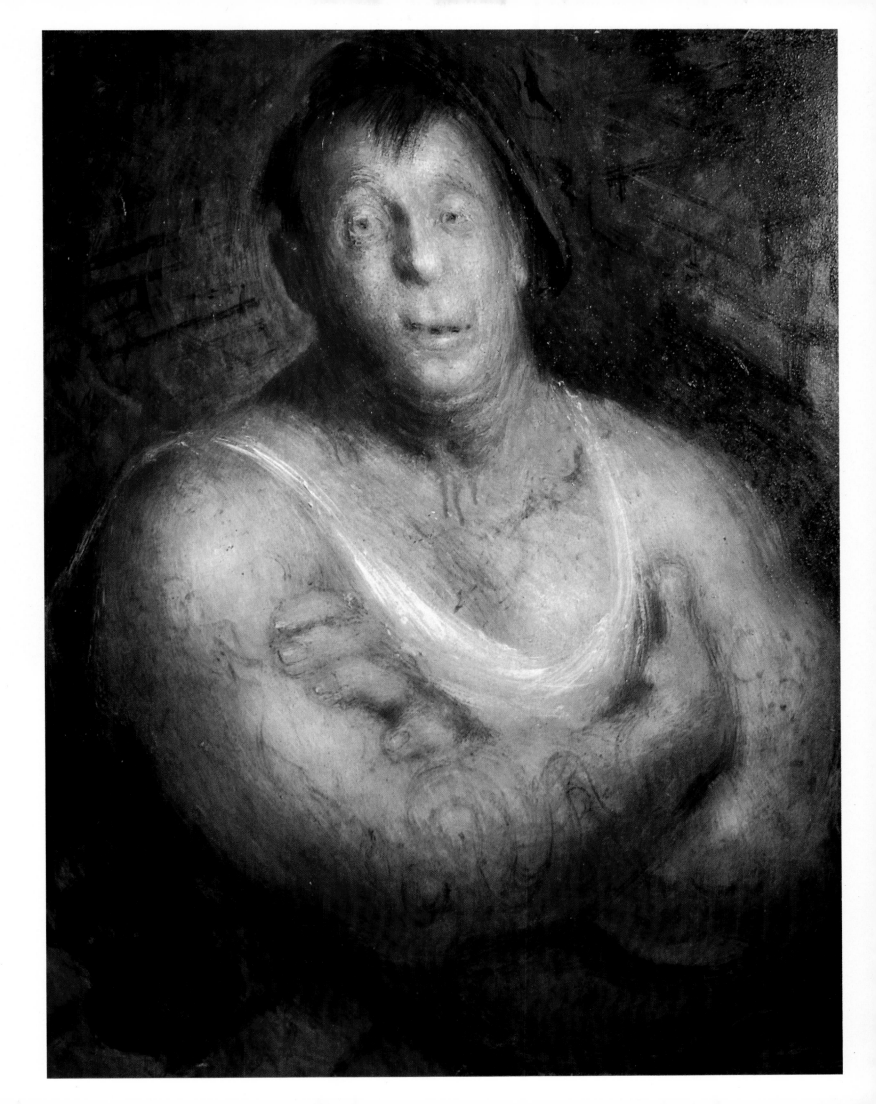

PLATE 53   Roland Wakelin *Ploughing at Hinton*

PLATE 54   Arthur Boyd *Wimmera Landscape*

PLATE 55   Russell Drysdale *The Ruins, Lake Callabonna*

NOTES ON THE PAINTINGS

PLATE 1   CONRAD MARTENS

Conrad Martens was born in London in 1801. His father was a German merchant and at one time was Austrian consul in London. Martens learned to paint with Copley Fielding but in 1816, when his father died, the family moved to Exeter. His connection with Australia began in 1832 when he sailed in the *Hyacinth* under the command of Captain Blackwood for a three-year voyage to India. However, in Rio de Janeiro he heard of a vacancy aboard the *Beagle* which was making a survey of the southern part of South America. Martens went aboard the ship at Montevideo and disembarked at Valparaiso in October 1832. During his time on board the *Beagle* he became friendly with Charles Darwin.

From South America, Martens sailed for Tahiti and later, Sydney, where he arrived in April 1835. For the next forty-three years he lived and painted around Sydney, travelling occasionally to various parts of the country. Like Turner, his paintings often depict romantic landscapes dominated by the sky or the weather. He made many paintings of Sydney Harbour, among which *Sydney from Vaucluse* is considered one of his most beautiful. Martens died in 1878.

PLATE 2   LOUIS BUVELOT

Abraham Louis Buvelot migrated to Australia from Switzerland in 1865, partly because he hoped that the climate would have a good effect on his health. Buvelot was born in Switzerland in 1814 and studied at Lausanne and Paris. For nearly twenty years he painted in Brazil under the patronage of Don Pedro II who provided him with a studio in his palace. He later went to the East Indies and India before ill health prompted him to emigrate to Australia.

Buvelot's work aroused no interest on his arrival in Melbourne, and he was forced to work as a photographer while his wife gave French lessons. His fortunes were restored when his work received favourable reviews from James Smith, critic for the *Argus*, who compared his landscapes to those of Millet and Corot.

Buvelot's paintings, of which the two examples reproduced in this book are typical, were forerunners of those which were to come from the 'Heidelberg School' of Roberts, Streeton, McCubbin and Co. These serene, open-air paintings have led to him being dubbed 'the Grandfather of Australian Landscape Painting'. He died in 1888.

PLATE 4   FREDERICK McCUBBIN

Frederick McCubbin was born in Melbourne in 1855 and died there in 1917. His father was a baker and for many years McCubbin was involved in the family business in West Melbourne (depicted in one of McCubbin's paintings). McCubbin studied drawing under Thomas Clark at an Artisan's School in Carlton, and later studied painting under Eugène von Guérard and George Folingsby at the National Gallery of Victoria. In 1885 he met Tom Roberts who had just returned from travelling in Europe, and together with Louis Abrahams they set up the first artists' camp at Box Hill, a bushland settlement east of Melbourne. In these surroundings, and later at nearby Blackburn, where he lived for a time, McCubbin painted some of his most famous works. *The Letter* was painted in 1886 and the model was Ann Moriarty whom McCubbin had met a short time earlier and who was later to become his wife. Ann Moriarty is also believed to have posed for the very similar painting, *A Summer Morning's Tiff* by Tom Roberts, which was painted at about the same time.

PLATE 5 TOM ROBERTS

The Artists' Camp 1886
oil on canvas 18 × 23⅞
National Gallery of Victoria,
Melbourne

Thomas William Roberts was born in Dorchester, England in 1856. He went to the local grammar school where he showed some talent for art, but when he was twelve his father died and his mother, whose brother lived in Australia, decided to emigrate. In Melbourne Roberts worked with a photographer at Collingwood and later for a city photographer, drawing decorative floral borders on photographs. One night a week he went to drawing classes at a school in Collingwood and in 1875 he won the drawing prize. The following year he went to evening classes at the National Gallery School and met, among others, Frederick McCubbin and Louis Abrahams. In the same year he held an exhibition of his work at the photographer's studio and made his first sale. Roberts later contributed to the Australian exhibit at the International Exhibition in Melbourne in 1880 when his work received favourable mention from James Smith, critic of the *Argus*.

In 1881 Roberts sailed for England and on arrival enrolled at a Royal Academy school. He later spent three years on a roving holiday through Europe which exhausted his finances. When offered a job by another Melbourne photographer he returned to Australia. In 1885–6 Roberts, Abrahams and McCubbin set up the first artists' camp at Box Hill. The camp was situated near Houston's farm, not far from the township which was then a bush settlement nine miles east of Melbourne. As a youth Roberts had visited an aunt who lived in the district and this was probably how he first came to know the blue-gum country around Box Hill. The central figure in *The Artists' Camp* was posed by Louis Abrahams, who also posed as the dejected pioneer in McCubbin's *Down on His Luck*.

PLATE 6 FREDERICK McCUBBIN

The Lost Child 1886
oil on canvas 45 × 28½
National Gallery of Victoria,
Melbourne

One of McCubbin's best-known works, *The Lost Child* was painted at the Box Hill camp shortly after it was set up. McCubbin frequently used models for his studies of bush life, which occasionally gave them a somewhat 'posed' appearance. *The Lost Child* is also typical of much of McCubbin's work in that, although it is a remarkable evocation of the Australian bushland, the general effect of the painting is to create a sombre mood, in which the monotony, rather than the freshness of the country is emphasised.

PLATE 7 GIROLAMO NERLI

The Voyagers
oil on pulpboard 12 × 21½
Art Gallery of New South
Wales, Sydney

PLATE 8
*The Beach at Port Melbourne
from the Foreshore, St Kilda*
oil on cardboard 8 × 16
National Gallery of Victoria,
Melbourne

Marchese Girolamo Ballatti Nerli was born in Sienna in 1863, the son of an Italian nobleman and an English mother. He arrived in Melbourne in 1886. Nerli studied in Florence but was strongly influenced by the French Impressionist painters, especially the early work of Monet. In turn this influence was transmitted through Nerli's Australian painting to the paintings to of Charles Conder and Arthur Streeton when the three artists were associated in Sydney in the 1890s.

Nerli later became director of the Dunedin, New Zealand, Art School, a post he held for three years. During World War I he was on the staff of the Italian embassy in London. He died at Nervi, near Genoa, in 1926.

The Voyagers makes an interesting comparison with Roberts' *Coming South*. Nerli's work, made about the same time, reveals how much closer he was to true impressionism than Roberts. *The Beach at Port Melbourne* was probably painted when Nerli was still in his mid-twenties, before he left for Sydney where many of his best works were done.

PLATE 9 — TOM ROBERTS

Coming South 1886
oil on canvas 25⅛ × 19⅞
National Gallery of Victoria,
Melbourne

Roberts made the original sketches for *Coming South* on board the *S.S. Lusitania* in 1885. This was the vessel which brought him back from his travels in Europe to a new job reorganising the Melbourne studio of photographers, Barrie and Brown. A 'social comment' work, *Coming South* effectively captures the mood of emigrants hopefully making their way to a new life in Australia.

PLATE 10 — ARTHUR STREETON

Golden Summer 1889
oil on canvas 32 × 60
Private Collection, Victoria

Arthur Streeton was born near Geelong, Victoria, in 1867, the fourth child of a teacher in the Victorian Education Department. Streeton left school to work in an importer's warehouse, and in 1884 he was attending drawing classes at the National Gallery School in Melbourne. In 1886 he got a job as an apprentice with the lithographic printers Troedel and Cooper and about this time got to know Frederick McCubbin who was teaching at the Gallery. In the summer of that year McCubbin met Streeton on the beach at Mentone, near Melbourne and, impressed with the seascape Streeton was painting, invited him to join the camp which Roberts, McCubbin and Abrahams had set up at Box Hill.

Not long after, Streeton gave up his job at the printery and went to paint at Templestowe with a colleague from the Gallery School, David Davies. The Davies family owned the Eaglemont Estate, near Heidelberg, and Davies' brother offered Streeton the use of a cottage there as a studio. The other members of the Box Hill group, with the exception of McCubbin, joined Streeton in the cottage which was to become the birthplace of the 'Heidelberg School'. It was here, in the Yarra Valley, that Streeton painted *Golden Summer* in 1888.

PLATE 11 — TOM ROBERTS

The Sunny South 1887
oil on canvas 12½ × 24⅛
National Gallery of Victoria,
Melbourne

Roberts painted at Mentone, a resort on Port Phillip Bay not far from Melbourne, in 1887 and 1888, when he camped with other members of the Box Hill group. *The Sunny South*, whose nude bathers were probably Roberts' fellow painters, makes an interesting contrast in both style and subject to Conder's *Holiday at Mentone* (1888). Roberts, Conder and Streeton frequently painted at Mentone or nearby Beaumaris or Sandringham during the hot summer months.

PLATE 12
A Summer Morning's Tiff
1887
oil on canvas 29¼ × 19¾
Ballarat Art Gallery, Victoria

Roberts' painting bears a superficial resemblance to Frederick McCubbin's *The Letter*. Both paintings were made in the period 1885–6 when Roberts, Streeton and Abrahams were camped at Box Hill. Ann Moriarty, who McCubbin had met at an artists' picnic at nearby Blackburn and who was to be the future Mrs Frederick McCubbin, is believed to have been the model for Roberts' painting as well as for *The Letter*.

PLATE 13 — CHARLES CONDER

Departure of the S.S. Orient
—*Circular Quay* 1888
oil on canvas 18 × 20
Art Gallery of New South
Wales, Sydney

Charles Conder was born in London in 1868, the son of a railway engineer. He had some training in art but his father did not approve of the boy's desire to become a painter, and in 1884 Conder was sent to Australia to be apprenticed to his uncle, a surveyor in the New South Wales Lands Department. Nevertheless, he went to evening art classes and got to know Julian Ashton, and in 1886 was employed as an illustrator on the *Illustrated Sydney News*. Several of the staff artists belonged to a group headed by Ashton and including Girolamo Nerli, which used to go on painting excursions, especially around the lower reaches of the Hawkesbury River and Sydney Harbour.

In the summer of 1888 Conder met Tom Roberts who had gone to Sydney in connection with illustrations he was doing for the *Picturesque Atlas of Australasia*. He painted with Roberts at Coogee and Bondi and a few months later, at Roberts' invitation, went to Melbourne to join Roberts and his colleagues at Box Hill.

The *Departure of the* S.S. Orient was painted when Conder was only twenty, yet it is ranked among his finest works. It was included among ten paintings he exhibited in 1888 at the Art Society of New South Wales and was one of four which were sold. It was bought by the National Art Gallery of New South Wales for twenty guineas.

Conder painted *Cove on the Hawkesbury* in 1888 when he was spending his spare time with Ashton's group. During this time his work was particularly influenced by the Impressionist style of Nerli.

PLATE 15   FREDERICK McCUBBIN

In 1889, when McCubbin painted *Down On His Luck* at Box Hill, he was living at Auburn, an inner Melbourne suburb, where he had settled after his marriage to the nineteen-year-old Ann Moriarty (Tom Roberts was best man). Three years earlier he had become teacher of drawing at the Melbourne National Gallery School (a post he was to hold for thirty-one years) and the family bakery business, which had taken much of his time, was sold.

Down On His Luck is another in McCubbin's bush genre series depicting the trials of pioneering life. The model for the dejected bushman was McCubbin's good friend Louis Abrahams. In the same year the first of McCubbin's seven children was born and named Louis.

PLATE 16   JULIAN ASHTON

Julian Ashton is better known today as a teacher (his pupils in later years included John Passmore and William Dobell) than as a painter. *The Prospector* is one of the more familiar of his works.

Ashton was born in Surrey, England, in 1851 and first worked in the civil engineering department of the Great Eastern Railway Company, although at the same time he had enrolled in classes at the Royal Academy and was illustrating children's books and magazines. After further studies in Paris he was offered a job as a staff artist on the *Illustrated Australian News* for which paper he and his brother George later covered the capture of Ned Kelly at Glenrowan. On arrival in Melbourne in 1878 he became friendly with the Swiss émigré Louis Buvelot and took an interest in the National Gallery School. Ashton moved to Sydney in 1883 and within a few years had gathered round him a circle which included Charles Conder, Girolamo Nerli and Henry Fullwood. His own work was showing a trend towards impressionism and he claimed to have made the first open-air painting in Australia. In 1889, following a chance meeting with Sir Henry Parkes, Ashton was elected a Trustee of the National Art Gallery of New South Wales where he was instrumental in increasing the purchase of Australian paintings. In the same year *The Prospector* was bought for the Gallery at the annual exhibition of the Artists' Society.

Six years later in 1895 he set up his own school, later known as the Sydney Art School, whose first star pupil was George Lambert. Ashton died at Bondi in 1942.

61

CHARLES CONDER

In October, 1888, Charles Conder left Sydney, where he had been working for the *Illustrated Sydney News*, and travelled to Melbourne to join the Box Hill group at the invitation of Tom Roberts. On his arrival, Roberts gave him accommodation in his new studio in Grosvenor Chambers and the two joined Streeton, McCubbin and Abrahams at Box Hill. Shortly afterwards they moved to Mentone, where Conder painted *Holiday at Mentone*, a work very reminiscent of the seaside paintings of the French Impressionists.

ARTHUR STREETON

About the time Streeton painted *Twilight Pastoral* the Box Hill group, of which he was a new member, shifted its camp near Houston's Farm to the cottage Streeton had obtained from the Davies family on Eaglemont Estate in the Yarra Valley. In the same year, 1889, Streeton exhibited forty paintings in the famous '9 × 5' exhibition which the Heidelberg group mounted in August. Streeton, who was twenty-two, had just been released from his indentures by the lithographic printers, Troedels and was painting full-time.

Not long after he painted *Twilight Pastoral*, Streeton produced another pastoral work at Eaglemont. The painting was originally titled *An Australian Gloaming*, but later Streeton changed the title, borrowing a line of Wordsworth's, to '*Still Glides the Stream and Shall Forever Glide*'. The work was exhibited at the Victorian Artists' Society Exhibition in 1890, and Frederick McCubbin took Julian Ashton (who was on a visit from Sydney) to see the show. As a result, the painting was bought by the National Art Gallery of New South Wales for seventy pounds. Encouraged by his success, Streeton decided to move to Sydney.

FREDERICK McCUBBIN

Frederick McCubbin did not abandon the Box Hill landscape when his colleagues moved to the cottage at Eaglemont, although he visited the cottage with Roberts at weekends. After his marriage in 1890 he and his wife lived first at Auburn, an inner suburb, then, in 1894, moved to Blackburn, a little beyond Box Hill. It was here, in the familiar blue-gum country, that McCubbin continued his series depicting the hardships of pioneering life with *A Bush Burial*.

Alexander Colquhoun, in his book on the artist, says that McCubbin painted *A Bush Burial* from life, even going so far as to make a small grave in his backyard and to pose his wife on the brink as the bereaved and grief-stricken widow.

ARTHUR STREETON

Streeton's impressionistic *The Settler's Hut* (also known as *Whelan on The Log*) is notable for the use of what Streeton called 'the real colours of the Australian landscape'. The work is said to reflect the influence of Streeton's association at this time with Charles Conder who, in the same year, painted a similar subject—a woodchopper by a tree under a bare sky—entitled, *Under a Southern Sky*.

PLATE 22

CHARLES CONDER

Not long after Conder painted *Yarding Sheep* and *Ricketts Point* in the summer of early 1890, the Eaglemont group disbanded—although Walter Withers and others were to continue painting in the area for some time. In April, as the Eaglemont painters dispersed, Conder sailed for London on the S.S. *Austral*, planning to study in Paris. His surveyor uncle in Sydney had paid Conder's fare and made him an annual allowance of one hundred and twenty pounds.

PLATE 23
*Ricketts Point, near
Sandringham* 1890
oil on canvas 12 × 30¼
National Gallery of Victoria,
Melbourne

After visiting Rome and Florence, he arrived in England, painted for a while, then moved to Paris where he enrolled at the Academy Julian and became friendly with William Rothenstein and Toulouse Lautrec. For some time, Conder's way of life had been what is usually termed 'dissolute', in fact it has been suggested that he had contracted syphilis in Australia. His new friends encouraged his excesses and, in 1891, he was forced to convalesce in Algeria. For the remaining years of his life (he was only twenty-two) he painted and made lithographs in Paris and London, moving in circles which included Aubrey Beardsley, William Sickert and Oscar Wilde. He married in 1901 and his wife had a steady income, but his health finally gave way in 1906 and, after several spells in sanatoria, he died in England in 1909 at the age of forty. Today Conder's work is much sought after in both Europe and Australia, bringing prices far in excess of those paid for the works of his Heidelberg colleagues.

PLATE 24

ARTHUR STREETON

Following the purchase of '*Still Glides the Stream*' by the National Art Gallery of New South Wales in 1890, Arthur Streeton moved to Sydney. He lived for a time at the artists' camp known as Curlew Camp at Little Sirius Cove on Sydney Harbour. Here Streeton lived with a mixed group including many non-artists, for twelve shillings and sixpence a week. During his time at the camp he made many paintings of harbour and beach scenes. Although the locality of this painting is not given, he had earlier painted several scenes at Coogee and he also painted regularly at Manly. Julian Ashton, who had organised the purchase of '*Still Glides the Stream*', wrote of Streeton in this year as 'a slim, debonair young man of about twenty-four years of age, with a little gold-pointed beard and fair complexion. When he wasn't painting he was quoting Keats and Shelley'.

PLATE 25

EMANUEL PHILLIPS FOX

Phillips Fox was born in Fitzroy, Melbourne in 1865, the son of a photographer. He trained at the National Gallery School and at twenty won a prize for landscape painting. Between 1887 and 1890, Phillips Fox studied in Paris. He exhibited there in 1890 at the Paris Salon. He returned to Melbourne the following year and subsequently held an exhibition. Together with Tudor St George Tucker, Phillips Fox conducted the Melbourne Art School from 1893 to 1902. A summer school was also held at 'Charterisville', Withers' former home at Heidelberg and the undated *Moonrise, Heidelberg* may have been painted at about this period. Many of Phillips Fox's paintings are markedly reminiscent of the leading French Impressionists, Monet, Renoir, Degas, but in his own time his influence was greater as a teacher than as a painter.

PLATE 26 FREDERICK McCUBBIN

In contrast to some of his contemporaries, McCubbin did not adopt the style of French Impressionism until after he had travelled to Europe in 1907. His earlier paintings, with their strong social themes, have a style somewhere between the early *plein air* painters like Buvelot and the true impressionist style. *The North Wind* is another of McCubbin's commentaries on pioneering life, but lacks the familiar Box Hill bushland setting.

PLATE 27 ALBERT HENRY FULLWOOD

Albert Henry Fullwood was one of the young artists who made up Julian Ashton's group in Sydney in the early 1890s. Born in Birmingham, England in 1863, Fullwood arrived in Australia in 1881 after having had some training at the Birmingham Institute. He later became an artist on the *Bulletin* and the *Picturesque Atlas of Australia*. He was among the group which Tom Roberts persuaded to secede from the Arts Society of New South Wales in 1898 to form the New South Wales Society of Artists. In 1900 he went to America and later to London, where he worked as a magazine illustrator. After World War I he was commissioned to paint pictures of the Western Front for the Australian War Memorial in Canberra. He returned to live in Australia in 1920 and died in 1930.

PLATE 28 TOM ROBERTS

In 1891 Tom Roberts spent six weeks travelling on outback stations in New South Wales with various sheep drovers. During this time he made several studies and sketches, and the painting *The Breakaway*, which his friend Arthur Streeton described as 'a masterpiece'. The painting combines elements of both realistic illustration and impressionism. It was exhibited in May 1892 at the first exhibition held at the new gallery of the Victorian Artists' Society in Albert Street and was favourably reviewed by James Smith, the *Argus* critic, who had been scathing about Roberts earlier and now famous work, *Shearing the Rams*.

PLATE 29 ARTHUR STREETON

Streeton painted '*Fire's On*' in the Blue Mountains of New South Wales in 1891. The scene--men at work blasting a tunnel through the mountain—represents a departure from the landscapes Streeton had been recording up to this time. Although it is not readily apparent at first glance, the painting actually depicts the body of a dead man being brought from the tunnel after a fatal accident. Streeton described the incident in a letter to Tom Roberts:

'Now I hear "Fire", Fire's ON in front from the gang close by, rest on my belly under the rock, take out my pipe and listen for the shots . . . boom and then rumbling of rock, the navvy under the rock with me and watching says MAN KILLED. He runs down the sheltered side and cries "Man Killed". Another takes it up and now it has run through the camp—more shots and crashing rock, we peep over and he lies all hidden bar his legs . . .'

About this time, Streeton was beginning to make trips on his own through the New South Wales countryside, without his companions of the Curlew Camp, in an effort to create 'something new'.

PLATE 30   GIROLAMO NERLI

A Wet Evening   1888
oil 12¾ × 15
Howard Hinton Collection,
Teacher's College,
Armidale, New South Wales

A Wet Evening is one of several wet evening street scenes of Sydney painted by Nerli and is reminiscent of similar works by the French Impressionist Monet.

PLATE 31   TOM ROBERTS

Portrait of Arthur Streeton
1891
oil on canvas 18⅛ × 14½
Art Gallery of New South
Wales, Sydney

Although best remembered for his portrayals of the Australian outback, Tom Roberts was a very fine portrait painter. The painting is inscribed, 'Smike Streeton aged 24'. 'Smike' was Streeton's nickname among the Box Hill group. Roberts was 'Bulldog' and McCubbin 'The Prof.' The portrait of Streeton was made in 1891 when both men were painting around Sydney and headquartered at Curlew Camp below what is now Taronga Park Zoo.

PLATE 32   WALTER WITHERS

A Bright Winter's Morn
1894
oil on canvas 24 × 36
National Gallery of Victoria,
Melbourne

Walter Withers was born in Staffordshire, England, in 1854. He studied in London and Paris before coming to Australia in 1882. On arrival, Withers packed a swag and spent the next eighteen motnhs working on the land. This brought him experience, but no money and he returned to Melbourne where a stationer by chance saw some of his sketches and bought them. Withers got a job as a draughtsman and also produced black and white portraits for sale. In his spare time he studied at the National Gallery of Victoria, where he may have met some of the Box Hill group.

In 1887 Withers returned to England and married. He then went to Paris, where he met Emmanuel Phillips Fox and studied at the Academy Julian. When his former employers offered him a job in Melbourne to illustrate *Chronicles of Early Melbourne* by Garryowen (Edmund Finn) Withers accepted, and in 1889 he joined Roberts, Streeton and Conder at Eaglemont. When the group moved out of the Eaglemont estate, Withers took over an old mansion, 'Charterisville', at Heidelberg, and let studios in the grounds to other artists. *A Bright Winter's Morn* is typical of the poetic treatment Withers gave to his subjects.

PLATE 33   ARTHUR STREETON

Boys Bathing, Heidelberg
1891
oil on canvas 12⅜ × 24¾
Queensland Art Gallery,
Brisbane

Between trips to Sydney and the Blue Mountains in 1891–2, Streeton had the use of Roberts' studio in Melbourne while Roberts was away travelling. *Boys Bathing* was almost certainly painted not far from the Eaglemont estate or 'Charterisville' where even today parts of the Yarra river are not so very different from when Streeton painted them eighty years ago.

PLATE 34   TOM ROBERTS

Eileen   1892
oil on canvas 19¼ × 14¼
Art Gallery of New South
Wales, Sydney

In 1892, after his travels in the New South Wales outback, Roberts decided to take a holiday. He embarked for a voyage on a fifteen-ton ketch which sailed north, visiting the Great Barrier Reef, New Guinea and northern islands. On his return in the spring of that year, he showed several works, at the Art Society of New South Wales' exhibition, where two of his small portraits, *Eileen* and *Head of an Aborigine* were bought for the National Art Gallery of New South Wales.

PLATE 35 DAVID DAVIES

Moonrise, Templestowe
1894
oil on canvas 46½ × 58⅜
National Gallery of Victoria,
Melbourne

David Davies was born in Ballarat in 1862 and studied at the Ballarat School of Design and later at the National Gallery of Victoria. In the late 1880s he painted with Streeton around Heidelberg and in 1890 he went to Europe where he spent three years in Paris studying. On his return in 1893 he went to live at Templestowe. Davies was one member of the Heidelberg group who did not have financial troubles. His family owned the extensive Eaglemont estate at Heidelberg on which stood the cottage which Davies' brother made available to the '9 × 5' painters. At Templestowe Davies painted his hauntingly beautiful landscapes including a series of 'moonscapes' of which *Moonrise, Templestowe*, is probably the best known. The soft shadowy colours of his nocturnal paintings are in contrast to the bright, sometimes harsh light of the Australian countryside depicted by his contemporaries.

Davies later moved to the bayside suburb of Cheltenham, but in 1897, returned to England. For a time he lived in Cornwall, but in 1908 went to France and he settled at Dieppe, where he remained for more than twenty years. He died in England in 1939.

PLATE 36 WALTER WITHERS

Mining Scene, Creswick
1893
oil on canvas 26¾ × 19¾
Ballarat Art Gallery, Victoria

In 1893 Walter Withers and his wife moved from the old Heidelberg mansion 'Charterisville'—at that time headquarters of an artists' 'colony'—to the town of Creswick, seventy-eight miles north-west of Melbourne on the western slopes of the Great Dividing Range. Creswick was a long-established gold-mining area, and Withers painted mining operations in the open air. He also conducted open-air painting classes and among those who attended were hometown youths Percy Lindsay and his young brother Norman. Withers returned to Heidelberg the following year.

PLATE 37 TOM ROBERTS

Bailed Up 1895–1927
oil on canvas 53 × 72
Art Gallery of New South
Wales, Sydney

Roberts' pursuit of realism reached its peak in his large painting *Bailed Up* which depicted the robbing of a Cobb & Co. mail coach by bushrangers in the 1860s. He is believed to have begun the painting in 1894 or 1895 when he was working in the sheep country of northern New South Wales in the district where the original incident occurred. Alan McCulloch, in *The Golden Age of Australian Painting*, tells how Roberts met the original driver of the coach which had been held up between Glen Innes and Inverell. In his zeal to re-create the incident, Roberts hired a similar coach, horses and models, and with instructions from the driver, arranged them all in a tableau of the original event. The scene was staged on a deserted road, and Roberts, in order to view the scene from the right perspective, built a platform, from which he painted, on the opposite side of the road.

The painting was exhibited at the first exhibition of the New South Wales Society of Artists in 1895 but was not sold and, for more than thirty years the painting remained in storage until, in 1927–8, Roberts brought it out and re-worked it. *Bailed Up* was exhibited at the Macquarie Galleries, Sydney, in June 1928. It was bought by J. W. Maund for five hundred guineas and placed on permanent loan to the National Art Gallery of New South Wales.

PLATE 38 EMANUEL PHILLIPS FOX

Art Students 1895
oil on canvas 72 × 45
Art Gallery of New South
Wales, Sydney

The critic James Gleeson has called this painting 'one of the most beautiful examples of impressionism in Australian painting'. It depicts Phillips Fox's own students at work in the Melbourne Art School, which Fox and his colleague from his Paris student days, Tudor St George Tucker, conducted between 1893 and 1902. Reminiscent of the style of Degas, the painting was indifferently received

66

when it was first exhibited at the Victorian Art Society in Melbourne in 1895. It remained unsold when Phillips Fox died in 1915 and was not purchased until 1943 when it was bought by the Art Gallery of New South Wales.

Ironically, Phillips Fox has been best known for many years for one of his lesser historical works, *The Landing of Captain Cook at Botany Bay, 1770*. It was commissioned in 1901 by the trustees of the National Gallery of Victoria and was bought from Phillips Fox for £500.

PLATE 39 WALTER WITHERS

The approaching storm, with its menacing sky and characteristic atmospheric light, was a subject which had a particular fascination for Withers, and his stylistic treatment is in marked contrast to the hard lights and clean brushstrokes of *Mining Scene*. *The Coming Storm* was painted in 1898, a year before a similar work, *The Storm*, painted in 1896, was to win the first Wynne Prize for landscape painting at the National Art Gallery of New South Wales. Withers was to win the prize again in 1900 with *Still Autumn*.

During the next twenty years, Withers became a respected figure in the art world of Victoria. He produced a series of *art nouveau* panels for the Manifold homestead at Camperdown, was elected President of the Victorian Artists' Society and was made a trustee of the National Gallery of Victoria. He died aged sixty in 1914.

PLATE 40 FREDERICK McCUBBIN

In 1895 the McCubbins moved from Blackburn to the bayside suburb of Brighton, but about the same time he also painted at Mount Macedon, thirty-six miles north-west of Melbourne. *Cottage, Macedon* shows a distinct change from his earlier bush genre paintings—although some of the best-known of these were yet to come—and gives a hint of McCubbin's later impressionist works.

PLATE 41 ARTHUR STREETON

This painting has remained one of the most popular of Streeton's works, possibly because it seems to represent a 'typical' or idealised view of the Australian landscape. Streeton painted *The Purple Noon* in 1896, after he had left the artists' camp at Sirius Cove and gone off inland to paint on his own. It depicts the upper reaches of the Hawkesbury River. Streeton had made his camp near the river and climbed a hill which had a commanding view of the scene. Here he built an awning to protect himself from the sun, and erected a large canvas held in place by stakes driven into the ground to form an outsize easel. He painted during the day and returned to his camp at night.

'*The Purple Noon's Transparent Might*' (the line is from a poem by Shelley) was shown in Streeton's first one-man exhibition in Melbourne in late 1896. 'It was completed', he wrote later 'with a kind of artistic intoxication with thoughts of Shelley in my mind'. The painting was an immediate success and was purchased by the National Gallery of Victoria for one hundred and fifty pounds. The reaction to the exhibition prompted Streeton to hold another the following year, and in 1898 he sailed for London.

The Old Inn was painted at Richmond on the upper reaches of the Hawkesbury, not far from where Streeton painted '*The Purple Noon's Transparent Might*'.

Two years later he arrived in London, where he worked hard but was unable to sell his paintings. In 1900 his *Sussex Landscape* was accepted by the Royal Academy and he subsequently visited Paris, but by 1905 he felt he could not make a living from his works and returned to Australia where he held another successful exhibition in Melbourne.

Streeton went back to London, married a Canadian, Nora Clench, and toured Europe. In 1918 he was a war artist and in 1920 he returned to live in South Yarra. In 1929, after more exhibitions and world travels, he was appointed art critic of the *Argus*. A Streeton retrospective exhibition was held in 1931 at the National Art Gallery of New South Wales and in 1937 he was knighted. He died at 'Long Acres', his home at Olinda in the Dandenong ranges, in 1943.

PLATE 43   # JOHN LONGSTAFF

Gippsland, Sunday Night,
February, 20th, 1898
oil on canvas 56½ × 78
National Gallery of Victoria,
Melbourne

John Longstaff was born at Clunes, Victoria, in 1862. He studied at the National Gallery of Victoria School, and was awarded the first Travelling Scholarship given by the school in 1887. This took him to France where he studied with such leading moderns as Toulouse Lautrec. Longstaff's own preference was for portraits and historical subjects, of which *Gippsland, Sunday Night* is representative. His most monumental work in this field was a painting of the explorers Burke, Wills and King which measures 111 × 169½. Longstaff was knighted in 1928. He had many commissioned portraits of Australian leaders and won the Archibald prize for artists. At one stage he was London representative for the trustees of the National Art Gallery of New South Wales. Among his best known works are *Lady in Black* and *Henry Lawson*. He died in 1941.

PLATE 44   # JULIAN ASHTON

The Selection   1913
oil on canvas
Newcastle City Art Gallery
Presented by Mrs I. Yates

The Selection was one of Julian Ashton's later works and demonstrates a marked difference in style from *The Prospector*. While it still retains a skilful blending of bright light and deep shadow it replaces a stilted and formal look with a free and impressionistic air.

PLATE 45   # FREDERICK McCUBBIN

The Pioneer   1904
triptych, oil on canvas 88 × 115⅞
overall
National Gallery of Victoria,
Melbourne

McCubbin's bush genre paintings reached their peak in the large and somewhat sentimental tryptich, *The Pioneers*. The painting was first exhibited in 1904 at a one man exhibition of McCubbin's held in the Atheneum Gallery, Melbourne. The show was not a success and most of the paintings, including *The Pioneers*, remained unsold. The following year McCubbin re-worked the painting, adding a distant view of Melbourne in the upper portion of the last panel. Negotiations to buy the work were begun with the trustees of the National Gallery of Victoria, but the trustees were almost equally divided as to whether or not to buy the work. The matter was not resolved until the end of 1906 when one of the principal opponents of the painting died and was replaced by the painter John Mather. The gallery finally bought the work for three hundred and fifty guineas and, partly as a result of the sale, McCubbin was able to make a long awaited trip abroad.

    The Pioneers was McCubbin's last big bush painting. He returned to Australia in 1908, feeling overwhelmed by the great European masterpieces he had seen, and from that time painted only small landscapes and street scenes in a style much more influenced by Turner and mainstream impressionism. He painted at his home in South Yarra and collaborated on a large book about his work which was published in 1916. He died at South Yarra the following year aged sixty-two.

PLATE 46 # RUPERT BUNNY

The Garden Bench c. 1915
oil on canvas 28¾ × 23¾
Art Gallery of New South
Wales, Sydney

Rupert Charles Wulsten Bunny was born in St Kilda, Melbourne in 1864. He studied at the National Gallery of Victoria School in the early 1880s, after giving up his earlier studies in civil engineering and architecture. In 1884 he went to Europe and stayed for a while in Austria before going to London. Later he exhibited in Paris and at the Royal Academy. Bunny lived and painted in France, especially in Provence, for many years. In 1904 the French Government bought one of his paintings for the Luxembourg Museum and Bunny was offered French citizenship and a job designing Gobelin tapestries, which he declined.

Bunny's work was strongly influenced by the Impressionists and other painters. In his later period he often painted allegorical subjects on a grand scale and was regarded by his contemporaries in Australia as avant garde. In 1911, when he was at the height of his fame, he visited Australia and held an exhibition. Although he returned to France he had two further one man exhibitions in Australia in 1923 and 1928. *The Garden Bench* was exhibited at the former show in Sydney and was purchased by the National Gallery of New South Wales. Bunny returned to live permanently in Australia in 1933 after the death of his wife and, between 1940 and 1946, held regular exhibitions in Sydney at which a number of his works were bought for State galleries. In 1946 the National Gallery of Victoria organised a large Rupert Bunny Retrospective exhibition which was the first loan exhibition of works by a living artist the gallery had held. Bunny died the following year.

PLATE 47 # ELIOTH GRUNER

Australian Landscape: After Frost
oil on canvas 18 x 24
National Collection, Canberra

*Reproduced with kind permission of
Perpetual Trustee Co. Ltd.*

Elioth Gruner was born in Gisborne, New Zealand in 1882 of Norwegian and Irish parents. He was brought to Australia in the following year and when he was only twelve began his training at Julian Ashton's school in Sydney. Gruner specialised in landscape painting but by the time he had finished his schooling impressionism was beginning to wane and the innovations it had produced were becoming conventions. Gruner exhibited at the Royal Academy and the Paris Salon and was manager of the exhibition of Australian art at the Royal Academy in 1923. He won the Wynne prize for landscape painting seven times and was one of the most popular and successful painters of the period between the two world wars. He died in Sydney in 1939.

PLATE 48 # HANS HEYSEN

Spring Early Morning 1917
watercolour on paper 12 × 11
Private Collection

It has been said that Hans Heysen was the first Australian painter to recognise the native Australian eucalypts as objects of beauty. Certainly, he looked at them more closely than anyone before or since, and throughout his long life as an active painter he never tired of them. Heysen painted mainly in the Mt Lofty and Flinders Ranges of South Australia and his watercolour work had such a characteristic and popular style that it inspired a host of imitators, most of whose work was inferior.

Heysen was born in Germany in 1877 and was brought to Adelaide by his parents when he was six years old. As a youth he was trained in Adelaide, and when he was twenty-two he went to France where he studied at the Academy Julian and the Ecole des Beaux Arts in Paris. He returned to Adelaide four years later and set up his own school of painting and drawing. Later he moved to Hahndorf in the Mt Lofty ranges, which was to be his home for the rest of his life. He was awarded the Wynne Prize for landscapes nine times and was knighted for his services to Australian painting. He died in 1970.

SALI HERMAN

Sali Herman was born in Zurich, Switzerland in 1898. He studied art in Zurich and Paris, and during the 1920s began dealing in art. Herman had travelled widely in Europe before he came to Australia in 1937. In Melbourne he was a student at George Bell's school and in 1944 he was awarded the Wynne prize for landscape painting. Herman was an official War Artist during World War II. His favourite subjects are street scenes in Sydney's older suburbs. His work is represented in all State galleries and in Australian legations overseas.

WILLIAM DOBELL

At the time of his death in 1970, William Dobell was Australia's best-known painter. Born in Newcastle, New South Wales, in 1899, he went to Sydney when he was twenty-five and began attending classes at Julian Ashton's School. In 1929 he was awarded the Society of Artists' Travelling Scholarship which enabled him to study at the Slade School, London, where he lived, apart from trips abroad, until 1938, when he returned to Australia.

Mrs South Kensington was painted towards the end of that period. It is not, strictly, a portrait from life, but a composite 'type', depicting a cold, dry, husk of a woman, and is regarded as one of Dobell's most successful works. In 1943 Dobell was awarded the Archibald Prize for portraiture, for his painting of his colleague Joshua Smith. The award caused a controversy and the painting was branded a caricature, prompting several protrait painters to take legal action to restrain the judges of the competition from awarding the prize to Dobell. The action was unsuccessful and Dobell subsequently won the Archibald again in 1948 with *Margaret Olley* and in 1960 for his portrait *Dr Edward McMahon*. Among Dobell's other significant awards were the Wynne Prize in 1948 and the *Australian Women's Weekly* Prize for portraiture in 1957. His portrait of Sir Robert Menzies for the cover of *Time* magazine in 1960 revived some of the old controversy about Dobell's portraits. He was knighted in 1966.

RUSSELL DRYSDALE

Probably no other modern Australian painter has been so successful in capturing the spirit of the Australian outback. Few, also, can match his popularity. Drysdale's *Moody's Pub*, and *The Drover's Wife* hang in bars, offices and lounge rooms throughout Australia.

George Russell Drysdale was born in Sussex, England in 1912 and came to Australia as a child. He first studied art at the George Bell school in Melbourne, then later in London and Paris. His work hangs in all Australian State galleries, the New York Metropolitan, the National Gallery of London and the National Gallery, Aberdeen. Retrospective exhibitions of Drysdale's paintings were held in New South Wales in 1960 and in Queensland in 1961. In 1962 Drysdale was appointed a member of the Commonwealth Art Advisory Board.

The Rabbiters is a typical Drysdale work, in which a basically realistic approach is given an almost surrealistic treatment. It was painted in 1947, three years after he made a tour of drought-stricken areas of New South Wales for the *Sydney Morning Herald*.

PLATE 52 # WILLIAM DOBELL

The term 'Billy Boy' is applied to the workman whose job is to boil the billy for morning and afternoon tea breaks. Dobell painted his portrait in 1943 when he was working on wartime camouflage at a Royal Australian Airforce base in New South Wales. The inspiration for the painting was an Irishman, Joe Westcott who, according to Dobell, who told James Gleeson, was more interested in talking politics than he was in making the tea.

PLATE 53 # ROLAND WAKELIN

Roland Shakespeare Wakelin was born at Greytown, New Zealand in 1887 and came to Australia in 1912. Later he visited Paris and London where he first came across the work of Cézanne which was to influence his own painting for some years. His respect for the French painter was demonstrated when he named his Sydney house 'Cézanne'. Returning to Australia, Wakelin exhibited his work at the Macquarie Galleries, Sydney and in 1935 was elected to the Society of Artists. Despite the early influence of Cézanne, Wakelin evolved his own romantic style and, together with a small group of other painters, became one of the first in Australia to experiment with post-impressionism. In 1947 he was awarded the Society of Artists' medal for services to Australian painting.

PLATE 54 # ARTHUR BOYD

Arthur Boyd was born in Murrumbeena, Melbourne in 1920. He had no formal training in painting and drawing but studied with his grandfather Arthur Merric Boyd, the New Zealand-born landscape painter who came to Australia in 1886. Arthur Boyd first exhibited in Melbourne in 1939 when his work was mainly impressionist landscapes and portraits. In 1959 Boyd went to England and held his first London exhibition the following year. Later, in 1961, he was commissioned to design the ballet decor for *Renard* performed at the Edinburgh Festival. This was followed by a retrospective exhibition at the Whitechapel Art Gallery in 1962. Boyd's paintings can be seen in all State galleries and in public and private collections in Europe and America.

PLATE 55 # RUSSELL DRYSDALE

Between 1957 and 1965 Drysdale made several painting trips to parts of Central and Western Australia. One of these took him to Lake Callabonna, a shallow lake 350 miles north-east of Adelaide, whose saline mud has yielded many fossils including the skeletons of prehistoric animals: a fitting location for one of Drysdale's dramatic and evocative outback studies.